PROGRAM DEVELOPMENT AND EVALUATION IN PREVENTION

Other Books in the Prevention Practice Kit

*To my family: Lynn, Suzanne and Pete, Zack, and our dog, Lucy.
And to Andy Horne, my good friend and fellow
trooper in prevention lo these many years.*

PROGRAM DEVELOPMENT AND EVALUATION IN PREVENTION

ROBERT K. CONYNE
University of Cincinnati

Los Angeles | London | New Delhi
Singapore | Washington DC

Los Angeles | London | New Delhi
Singapore | Washington DC

FOR INFORMATION:

SAGE Publications, Inc.
2455 Teller Road
Thousand Oaks, California 91320
E-mail: order@sagepub.com

SAGE Publications Ltd.
1 Oliver's Yard
55 City Road
London EC1Y 1SP
United Kingdom

SAGE Publications India Pvt. Ltd.
B 1/I 1 Mohan Cooperative Industrial Area
Mathura Road, New Delhi 110 044
India

SAGE Publications Asia-Pacific Pte. Ltd.
3 Church Street
#10-04 Samsung Hub
Singapore 049483

Acquisitions Editor: Kassie Graves
Editorial Assistant: Elizabeth Luizzi
Production Editor: Brittany Bauhaus
Copy Editor: QuADS Prepress (P) Ltd.
Typesetter: C&M Digitals (P) Ltd.
Proofreader: Jeff Bryant
Indexer: Diggs Publication Services, Inc.
Cover Designer: Glenn Vogel
Marketing Manager: Lisa Sheldon Brown
Permissions Editor: Adele Hutchinson

Copyright © 2013 by SAGE Publications, Inc.

Printed in the United States of America

Library of Congress Cataloging-in-Publication Data

Program development and evaluation in prevention / editor, Robert K. Conyne.

p. cm. — (Prevention practice kit)
Includes bibliographical references and index.

ISBN 978-1-4522-5801-0 (pbk.)

1. Preventive health services—Planning. 2. Medicine, Preventive. 3. Medical policy. I. Conyne, Robert K.

RA427.8.P762 2013
362.1—dc23   2012040377

This book is printed on acid-free paper.

12 13 14 15 16 10 9 8 7 6 5 4 3 2 1

Brief Contents _____

Detailed Contents _____

Acknowledgments_____

Thanks to Kim Bolen and to Kat Raczynski for all your assistance and to Lynn Rapin, all the University of Cincinnati students, and organizational consultees who have helped refine the model described in this book.

1 Introduction to Program Development and Evaluation in Prevention

Why does this *Kit* on prevention practices contain a book on program development and evaluation? The following five points underscore its importance.

Prevention Occurs Through Programs Applied Early

Prevention goals are accomplished through intentional and effective *programs* that are applied prior to entrenched dysfunctions appearing in a targeted population. So if programs are the means through which prevention is accomplished, then it is necessary to know how to develop and evaluate these programs. This reasoning explains the existence of this book on program development and evaluation (PD&E).

Programs are sometimes preceded by adjectives such as "intervention," "treatment," and "prevention." We are interested in this *Kit*, of course, in prevention programs.

Parenthetically, I will make no attempt in this book to provide a detailed discussion of prevention, although it obviously needs to be understood in order to deliver PD&E of prevention programs. Other books in this *Kit* are focused specifically on this task. I will refer you to them and to other relevant sources about prevention for reference (e.g., Albee, 1985; Gullotta & Bloom, 2003; Hage et al., 2007; Kenny, Horne, Orpinas, & Reese, 2009; Romano & Hage, 2000), including two of my own contributions (Conyne, 2004, 2010). The latter book is devoted to prevention PD&E and contains considerably more information in depth than is possible to present here, especially regarding the role of incidence reduction in prevention programs. This current book is not a condensed version of its predecessor, but a companion text, as it takes a complementary but different approach to processes of PD&E.

Let's now return to the discussion of prevention occurring through programs. Metaphorically, a program can be thought of as the engine that powers an intervention or prevention train. These programs can vary widely in scope and complexity: from a personal prevention program, where an individual learns and practices yoga to reduce and manage stress and to gain a sense of personal mastery, to a national wellness program aimed at eradicating obesity in children and promoting a healthier way of life. A key element of all programs, regardless of scope, is that they need to be intentionally organized, delivered, and practiced. They should possess a theoretical or conceptual base, have a framework and plan for implementation, and be followed faithfully and consistently with progress charted in some useful way.

Note that what may on the surface appear to be simple or easy to achieve in terms of prevention, such as establishing a personal yoga practice mentioned above, usually proves to be much more challenging. Here is another case in point. Heart disease and strokes are two of the nation's most deadly and costly health concerns. Because of the large contribution of personal lifestyle that frequently attends these and many other chronic health concerns, these conditions are highly susceptible to prevention. The preventive strategies are knowable and include dietary change, daily physical activity, stopping smoking, controlling cholesterol and high blood pressure, and taking a "baby" aspirin daily if recommended by one's medical doctor (Office of Disease Prevention and Health Promotion, 2011). Even though being knowable, however, actually enacting these strategies consistently is often an entirely different matter, much like the low success rate associated with New Year's resolutions. In fact, what each of these strategies needs is to be embedded within a PD&E plan that can be monitored and followed regularly.

Prevention programs are unique because they are provided to help people and systems avoid dysfunctions, disorders, and other forms of serious problems. As pointed out decades ago (Albee, 1982; Albee & Gullotta, 1997), effective prevention programs are the only way to lower the number of *new* cases of a disorder or the *rate* of development of these new cases from occurring because these programs are implemented *before-the-fact*, prior to the disorder becoming set. In public health terms, this approach is known as incidence reduction.

Thus, prevention programs are conducted with the overarching goal of lowering the incidence of a disorder among members of a targeted population (Coie et al., 1993) According to the Institute of Medicine model (1994), prevention programs may be offered to all members of a population, regardless of health or risk ("universal" form of prevention), to a subset of it who are at risk ("selective" form of prevention), or to another subset who evidence early signs of a disorder but are not yet able to be diagnosed ("indicated" form of prevention). In any case, prevention programs are delivered purposefully to develop or enhance strengths in people and systems (the term *systems* refers, in this instance, to organized environments found in work, family, school, community, etc.), while seeking to reduce known stressors. Including this combination of components within a prevention program of *buttressing strengths* (e.g., social connections and support, competencies, and self-esteem) while *decreasing deficits* (e.g., stressors, social isolation, poverty, crime, oppression, and racism), when introduced appropriately to people before they have already succumbed to serious health issues (e.g., depression), position the program to produce preventive effects (Albee, 1982; Conyne, 2004, 2010). This kind of approach is known as *incidence reduction*, which Albee maintained was the one and only way to thwart the emergence of new cases of any disorder in a population.

The personal and societal costs of mental problems are immense. Over the course of a lifetime, the prevalence rate of adults in the United States meeting the criteria for a diagnosable mental illness is estimated at 50% (Kessler et al., 2008). In terms of incidence, which is the particular concern of prevention, about 25% of the U.S. adult population and 10% of children and adolescents suffer from a diagnosable mental illness (Center for Disease Control and Prevention, 2005; U.S. Public Health Service, 2000). These figures do not include the far broader categories of mental health problems (where depth and intensity of disturbance do not reach a diagnosable stage but are often no less toxic), or those living a languished life, barely slogging through their days (Keyes, 2002, puts this at about 12%). The overall cost of mental health problems, including productivity losses and treatment expenses, is estimated at $247 billion per year (Wells, Mance, Tirmazi, & Gone, 2010). Sound programs of prevention are sorely needed.

As described by Cohen, Chavez, and Chehimi (2010), prevention exists along a spectrum. This spectrum provides a "systematic framework for developing effective and sustainable primary prevention programs" (p. 17).

Six levels are contained in this spectrum: (1) strengthening individual knowledge and skills, (2) promoting community education, (3) educating providers, (4) fostering conditions and networks, (5) changing organizational practices, and (6) influencing policy and legislation. Each of these levels can become the focus for the development of prevention programs.

A Program Comprises Interrelated Elements Existing Within an Open System

So a program is essential to prevention, but just what is a program, anyway? As already pointed out, we are concerned with particular kinds of programs, those that are connected to mental health and education, usually tagged as intervention, treatment, counseling, training, psychoeducation, and related forms of helping.

In a basic understanding of the term, a program has been defined as "a prearranged set of activities designed to achieve a stated set of goals and objectives" (Netting, Kettner, & McMurtry, 2008, cited in Kettner, Moroney, & Martin, 2008, p. 9). Such programs consist of an interrelated, open system of elements (Board of Regents, University of Wisconsin System, 2008; Chen, 2005; Stufflebeam, 2003): (a) context, (b) inputs, (c) transformative processes, (d) outputs, (e) impacts, (f) environment, and (g) feedback. These seven elements are dynamic, naturally open to mutual influence with the potential to be adapted through feedback (Conyne, 2010; Holden & Zimmerman, 2009).

Let's take a quick look at each part of a program's system of interrelationships.

Context: Every program or program waiting to be created is surrounded (Conyne, 2010) by its context. The context precedes and continually informs a program which, in turn, becomes another piece of the context over time. Thus, the context is a continual influencer of any program, and it also is influenced by the program.

A context is made up of its politics, culture, history, resources and constraints, and the values, needs, and interests of people within it (Patton, 1997). In a broader sense, to understand a context, it is necessary to assess its organizational, cultural, and political environment, to define the relationship that exists between program staff and constituents, and then to fit PD&E appropriately within situational resources and constraints.

Inputs: Inputs are resources acquired from the environment. These are the "raw stuff" needed to create and drive a program and to run its engine. Inputs include materials and equipment, facilities, personnel, capital, money, people, technology, time, and motivation—both tangible and intangible resources that are required for the program to operate.

Transformational processes: In a living organism, food is taken in, digested, and converted to energy and actions. This series of events can be referred to as transformational processes, where inputs are converted through a series of activities into outputs. In a program, transformational processes are found in program development plans that are used to intentionally guide the expenditure of resources into desired products. An ongoing series of training workshops (outputs), for instance, results from a collection of inputs, such as money, facilities, technology, trainers, and more that is guided by a program development plan.

Outputs: Any program is created to produce outputs, or products. Outputs are yielded by transformational processes. In mental health, prevention, and education, these outputs typically are "soft" ones, not the "hard" ones (e.g., automobiles, computers, butter—you get the idea) that might first spring to mind when hearing the term. So mental health programs are intended to produce such outputs as more or different knowledge, new skills, more positive attitudes, and coherent and ethical values and behaviors. In the realm of prevention, for instance, outputs coalesce around wellness and life skills competencies (e.g., parenting skills) and social justice and system change strategies (e.g., advocacy initiatives).

Impacts: Programs are intended to make observable differences in lives and in communities. An "impact" can be thought of as the "effect of an outcome." That is, did an attained outcome such as increased knowledge about parenting, or another about gaining new parenting skills, actually contribute to a change in the condition of better parenting, as determined by happier children, or by fewer missed school days, or by improved communication among family members? Impacts are measurable changes in program participants and/or the community environment that can be shown to have resulted from the program being implemented.

Environment: A program acts on its environment and is acted on by it. The *context* of a program, previously discussed, is the surroundings within which the program is developed and is nested. The *environment* of a program is what is affected by a program's implementation and, in turn, comprises the external world that shapes and influences a program's continued implementation. For instance, a community-wide family health program produces outputs and impacts that are, in turn, applied within the environment. Learned strategies are tried out with others in the family environment, and the larger national environment influences new practices through changing conceptions of what may constitute a "modern American family." Thus, a program exists in an open system of mutual and ongoing influences.

Feedback: The open system of a well-designed program is characterized by recurring feedback loops yielding information that, in turn, can be drawn on to help keep the program on track. Opportunities for feedback and its usability can be increased through careful planning and monitoring, which are two critically important aspects of PD&E. Feedback procedures can be designed to inform program managers with a flow of information about the appropriateness and adequacy of inputs and implementation so that alterations can be made or the equilibrium maintained, as warranted.

PD&E Involves Cyclical Phases of Planning, Implementation, and Effects, While Being Infused by the Processes of Community, Collaboration, and Cultural Relevance

In general, PD&E can be thought of as consisting of planning, implementation, and effects phases, which influence and inform each other in a cyclical way. So planning informs the other two phases, and they, in turn, each inform and influence one another. In real-world practice, it is to be expected that plans will be revised as events occur, that implementation will be continually readjusted in response to feedback, and that evaluation will be conducted all the way through the PD&E process and not left only to the end. Yet broad and distinguishable phases can be found in PD&E, and it is useful to consider them for teaching, learning, and even for delivery purposes.

I have placed (Conyne, 2010) considerable emphasis on the importance of three processes in prevention-oriented PD&E, what I labeled as the "Three Cs": (1) Community-based, (2) Collaborative, and (3) Culturally relevant. Prevention programs are typically set within systems, settings, and communities of some complexity; in short, these programs are community based. To be effective, prevention programs also demand the support and engagement of community stakeholders. "Preventionists" avoid doing things *to* people in favor of working *with* them. Prevention programs need to be planned, delivered, and evaluated with a cooperative, coparticipative ethic clearly articulated by words and deeds. Obtaining the active participation of stakeholders depends on many factors and issues, not the least of which are the abilities of professional staff to understand and honor the unique culture of participants and to collaborate with them effectively to yield mutually desirable outcomes.

Integrating the three Cs throughout the prevention PD&E process requires intention and concerted action to lay the proper groundwork for designing, conducting, and evaluating a prevention program. This groundwork rests on a foundation of "teamwork in action," where sharing, bridging, connecting, collaborating, engaging, and creating together are dominant activities. As I mentioned above, considerable attention had been given to this important area previously, so I will cover it only briefly in this book; however, please refer to Conyne (2010) for information.

Conducting Prevention PD&E Relies on Both Technical and People Skills

Effective conduct of PD&E depends on the technical and scientific acumen of experts, the natural experience and knowledge of members of the targeted population, and the development of positive interpersonal and group competencies and processes occurring between these two parties, and others, over time. In short, both technical and people skills are mandatory.

I developed and taught a graduate course in PD&E in Counseling, and another in Preventive Counseling, for decades. Without fail, when students come into the first of these courses they think stereotypically that all their people skills will be unimportant or, at best, neutralized in this course. They wrongly assume that PD&E requires only technical, scientific, and research and evaluation skills. As a consequence, because many (but not all) counseling students tend to be wary of research and evaluation functions, they enter the course with trepidation. One of my jobs as an instructor is to teach and to show students through practical experience in the course that all of their people skills and counseling training are fundamentally important for conducting PD&E successfully. They learn that PD&E is at its roots a people-driven set of procedures and processes, where positive listening skills, empathic understanding, and group facilitation skills—to mention just three areas—play a central role. So we start with and continue to work with that awareness throughout the course.

As well, PD&E also demands technical competencies, most certainly. One of the most challenging tasks in the overall PD&E process, which we will examine later in this book, is located at what is one of its earliest and most important steps: define the problem. Students grapple with this step, often having to return to it a few times as they move forward to subsequent steps, such as developing an evaluation design, in order to redefine and define again a more accurate and attainable problem. Engaging in this step demands patience, the ability to think through and to analyze data and information, and, if they are working with a team (as is often the case), to manage team dynamics productively.

Because the PD&E procedure involves a series of linked steps, each of which can become complex, being able to organize and manage information and data are essential. Computer skills, mapping, and scheduling systems, such as the Performance Evaluation Review Technique or the Gantt technique (Craig, 1978), are useful for organizing objectives, strategies, activities, tasks, responsibilities, resources, timelines, and evaluation methods.

Interpersonal, group, and collaborative decision-making competencies and processes also are critically important for PD&E. These are rightfully viewed as a subset of people skills, which were mentioned above. A naturally occurring discrepancy frequently is found in the field existing between prevention professionals ("experts in prevention") and community participants ("stakeholders in the local community"). In reality, both parties hold their own specialized sets of expertise; the professionals bring with them knowledge of prevention content and process, skills, experience, and sometimes resources (e.g., grant funding or access to technological assistance), while the local stakeholders embody life experience within the setting or the circumstance and with other members of the population that the eventual program will address. Being able to bridge the gap through effective use of collaboration skills is vital to success in PD&E efforts.

Effective Programs Depend on Sound PD&E Processes That Are Guided by an Overall Organizational Development and Evaluation Plan

As Yogi Berra, the Hall of Fame New York Yankee catcher and accidental "everyday philosopher," is credited with observing, "If you don't know where you're going how are you gonna know when you get there?" (Board of Regents, 2008, slide 6). A PD&E plan might please Yogi because in it planners have developed a detailed road map, routing activities toward goal accomplishment over time. A corollary to Yogi's observation points to one of the values of a PD&E plan as activities occur and feedback accrues relevant to progress: "The more you know about where you're going, the closer you are to being there" Craig, 1978).

The credible application of sound PD&E processes, guided by an overall PD&E plan, makes effective prevention programs possible. Moving through activities while being able to examine ongoing feedback regarding how they are being delivered (process) and their effect (outcome) affords program planners opportunities to make any needed adjustments and to reinforce what already seems to be working—while being open to new opportunities.

As a program nears its ending, questions about its effectiveness abound. If the program planners have been smart about it, they have been collecting evaluation data all the way through, not leaving the task only until the end.

But still, at the end, all involved will be looking for data to indicate if the program reached its goals and at what level.

So everyone discovers if the program was targeted well, had the right stuff, and made a difference. Did academic grades improve because of the program? Was domestic violence averted? Did participants behave more civilly? Were new cases of depression decreased? Or did fewer cases of depression develop?

Learning Exercise 1: Understanding PD&E

The following two quotations served to close out Chapter 1, which contained introductory material about PD&E:

"If you don't know where you're going how are you gonna know when you get there?"

and

"The more you know about where you're going, the closer you are to being there."

Write a paragraph about each quote explaining their connection with PD&E. Be specific.

Quote 1:

_____

_____

_____

_____

_____

_____

Quote 2:

_____

_____

_____

_____

_____

_____

Summary

This introductory chapter establishes a foundation for why PD&E is necessary for prevention. Five key aspects of PD&E in prevention are discussed here:

1. Prevention occurs through programs that are applied early.

2. A program comprises interrelated elements existing within an open system.

3. PD&E involves cyclical phases of planning, implementation, and effects, while being infused by the processes of community, collaboration, and cultural relevance.

4. Conducing prevention of PD&E relies on both technical *and* people skills.

5. Effective programs depend on sound PD&E processes that are guided by an overall PD&E plan.

We now turn our attention to background theory and concepts. You can find a more extensive and detailed discussion of the information that follows by referring to Conyne (2010), *Prevention* PD&E: *An Incidence Reduction, Culturally Relevant Approach*.

2

Background

Sources of Influence for PD&E in Prevention

PD&E in prevention is influenced by three main sources: (1) the fields of program evaluation and evaluation research; (2) community-based, collaborative, and culturally relevant approaches; and (3) evidence-based practice (EBP). These sources are the focus of Chapter 2. Again, see Conyne (2010) for more detail.

The Fields of Program Evaluation and Evaluation Research

PD&E emerges from the broad fields of program evaluation and evaluation research, which contain a variety of theories and models that are supported by scholarly research and publications. These fields are far too vast to be focused on in this book. Rather, I draw from them selectively some models and approaches that provide a good fit with PD&E for prevention.

Logic Model

The logic model presents a set of assumptions and "if-then" relationships that undergird many program and development models (Board of Regents, University of Wisconsin System, 2008; Kettner et al., 2008; Savaya & Waysman, 2005). It emphasizes the theory of PD&E and a focus on effectiveness, and it represents a kind of "road map" of how to proceed. The Logic Model adopts a systems-based framework for use in the development and evaluation of programs. It proceeds from inputs through process, outputs, and outcomes to impact. Use of a sequenced flow model such as this allows program planners and evaluators to define, address, and evaluate a problem in a rational and organized manner while recognizing that a program is essentially a system of interrelated parts. In this book, I will draw extensively from the Logic Model.

PRECEDE–PRODEED Model

This model (Green, 2007; Green & Kreuter, 1999) contains a comprehensive framework for assessing health and quality of life needs (PRECEDE) and for creating, delivering, and evaluating health promotion and other public health program intended to meet those needs (PROCEED). This model's attention to ecological variables within an informed, cyclical approach, coupled with its public health orientation, lends itself well to prevention.

Utilization-Focused Evaluation

This comprehensive approach is centered on the application of program evaluation findings by intended users, a focus that permeates it from beginning to end (Patton, 1997). The emphasis on involving stakeholder and primary users of program design and evaluation throughout the entire process of utilization-focused evaluation is an important contribution as it sets the table for collaborative processes.

Context–Input–Process–Product Model

This comprehensive model considers formative and summative evaluation of programs according to four major elements: context, input, process, and product, with product organized by impact, effectiveness, sustainability, and transportability (Stufflebeam, 2003). The completeness, directionality (beginning with context through transportability), and systems perspective of a multistage context–input–process–product (CIPP) evaluation is strategically valuable as is the incorporation of ecologically oriented concepts (context and sustainability).

Differential Social Program Evaluation

This framework (Tripodi, Fellin, & Epstein, 1978) indicates that social programs be evaluated by asking different questions timed to evolving program development stages (program initiation, program contact, and program implementation) and to distinct program evaluation stages (efforts, effectiveness, and efficiency). Specifying relationships between program development and program evaluation stages, along with sensitive questions timed for developmental progress in each of these stages, provides for clarity and promotes effectiveness.

Effectiveness-Based Program Planning

As mentioned earlier, this approach emerges from the Logic Model, and it stresses the importance of theory in an organized, systemic approach to program design and management (Kettner et al., 2008). Also, it emphasizes the importance of monitoring in program planning, where programs are subjected to adequate and ongoing assessment. This commitment to effectiveness is intended to provide both a rich database for program decision making as well as services to clients that can be continually improved.

HIP Pocket Guide to Planning and Evaluation

Specific PD&E steps are defined that are based on usefulness and feasibility for application in daily circumstances (Craig, 1978). The "HIP" designation is meant to convey the model's ease of use, simple enough that it could be carried in one's hip pocket. Six steps comprise this approach: (1) define the problem, (2) set the objective, (3) choose among alternative strategies, (4) prepare for implementation, (5) design the evaluation, and (6) use evaluation information. In Conyne (2010), I drew extensively from the *HIP* model.

Collaborative for Academic, Social, and Emotional Learning Implementation Cycle for Socioemotional Learning

Ten steps are detailed for implementing socioemotional learning (SEL; The Collaborative for Academic, Social, and Emotional Learning [CASEL], 2003, 2008; Devaney, O'Brien, Resnik, Keister, & Weissberg, 2006) to transform leadership in a school (Elias, O'Brien, & Weissberg, 2006). These are (1) commit to schoolwide SEL, (2) engage stakeholders to form a steering committee, (3) create and articulate a shared vision, (4) conduct needs assessment and identify what already is working well, (5) develop an action plan, (6) select evidence-based programs and strategies, (7) conduct initial staff development, (8) provide socioemotive skills instruction in classrooms, (9) expand to whole school, (10) revisit and adjust. The overall set of steps and especially specification of commitment, engagement, visioning, and the incorporation of evidence-based approaches are welcomed contributions.

Student Service Program Development Model

This tested model was part of the Western Interstate Commission for Higher Education initiative for improving mental health services on western campuses (Moore & Delworth, 1976). The program development model contains five stages: (1) getting the team formed and generating ideas using the Counseling Cube (Morrill, Oetting, & Hurst, 1974); (2) core planning and development; (3) pilot testing and deciding on offering; (4) training and delivery procedures, program evaluation; and (5) program maintenance and spin offs.

Transformative Research and Evaluation

In this approach (Mertens, 2008), evaluation is conceptualized within a social justice framework. Research questions and issues are developed within the context of marginalized communities and by giving credence to community needs and evaluator–community partnerships.

The Role of Community, Collaboration, and _____ Cultural Relevance for PD&E in Prevention

The importance of attending to community, collaboration, and cultural relevance, which I've abbreviated as the "three Cs" in PD&E, was introduced earlier. Now I will expand on this recommendation.

As we have seen, PD&E emerged as a practical application from the general discipline of program evaluation research, influenced by several different sources. It draws on systematically organized methods for creating, delivering, managing, and evaluating interventions and preventive programs.

Even though various models and methods are available for use, however, success is not guaranteed. Too many programs have failed during development and are never brought to trial, are ineffective due to low participation and support, or, when completed, are not sustained or adopted elsewhere (Wandersman & Florin, 2003).

Many reasons exist to explain these disappointments, including the following: improper understanding of the problem to be addressed, vague objectives, inadequate resources, confused responsibilities, muddled timelines, inadequate program monitoring, and insufficient attention to the usability of evaluation results—to list a few of the common but major culprits. Design and application of any PD&E model needs to delimit these kinds of threats.

While acknowledging and accepting all the above challenges to PD&E, it is my contention that an essential—and far too frequently overlooked—reason for the failure of many programs can be traced to the inability of program personnel to genuinely collaborate with community members, coupled with giving little or no attention to aspects of community and participant values and culture. Ignoring or being ineffective at making these kinds of community connections, in turn, contributes strongly to the creation of weakly positive, neutral, or sometimes even harmful programs.

Therefore, PD&E can be improved by incorporating more attention to community and culturally relevant processes. Doing so is especially important for application for prevention programs, where best practice mandates a community-based, culturally relevant, and collaborative approach (Hage et al., 2007).

The good news here is that attention to community, collaboration, and culturally relevant processes is not alien to some existing PD&E approaches. As examples, see the steps for community health assessment in PRECEDE–PROCEED, attention to context and sustainability in CIPP, and engaging stakeholders in CASEL. However, community involvement and cultural relevance are of such importance for enhancing readiness, involvement, satisfaction, adoption, success, and sustainability that they need to be centralized and prioritized within all PD&E initiatives. As I have already stressed, the preceding assertion especially is true when prevention programs are involved.

Community

"Community" represents a level of mental health program intervention that is unique. Much more typically occurring are interventions aimed at individual and group levels. Such community-level interventions are exemplified by individual counseling and therapy and by varieties of group work, including group counseling and psychotherapy, psychoeducation groups, and others. The community level, by contrast, is geared toward large numbers of people, including a population, existing within their natural setting. Examples include all community members in a city, students within a school, and employees of an organization, to name just three. In all cases, the focus is not on individuals taken separately, but on the entire population, or an identified subpopulation (e.g., one at higher risk) within the identified setting. In turn, the intervention or the prevention program is located within the community, it takes root and is delivered there, rather than asking people to leave their setting to be involved with the program somewhere else.

Conducting programs within a community-level setting has both benefits and drawbacks, just as is the case with any intervention choice. This makes for a rich but "messy" experience, a blending of a blessing and a curse. External validity of the program is improved because its location is in the actual setting, where real, genuine, and ongoing dynamics and conditions are at play, such as historical, economic, political, and cultural forces. Internal validity is reduced with community-level programs because the real-world setting diminishes the opportunity for program variables to be controlled and manipulated by program personnel.

Collaboration

Lamentably, in typical practice, the application of PD&E tends to be controlled by program personnel. Research, goals, methods, delivery, and evaluation too frequently are parachuted by program personnel down into a community and enacted without the participation and support of community members. That is, community participants often are not provided the opportunity to provide input or to engage in decision making that is central to the creation and delivery of a program. Thus, it is not "theirs," they do not own it, and regardless how sound its principles may be otherwise, without the investiture of community members in it, the program's chances of success are limited.

The antidote to this state of affairs is to find ways to meaningfully engage with community members throughout the PD&E process (Rollnick & Miller, 1995). Incidentally, for counseling, psychology, social work, and other mental health practitioners, connecting and engaging with people are the strength and focus of training programs (Smith, 2006). So finding engagement, an important process for PD&E, should be very good news, indeed, for mental health professionals.

A primary means for engagement is found in collaboration, which is a bilateral and coequal process of exchange and communication where members of each side of a transaction bring something of particular value; in a very real sense, a copartnership evolves (Elden & Levin, 1991). As I mentioned before, community participants bring to collaboration their life experience within the setting, while program personnel bring expert content knowledge and skills in developing and evaluating programs. Combining these two sets of knowing and doing can yield advances that would be difficult to attain by sole reliance on one or the other.

Taking a closer look at collaborating with community participants, when effected in all phases of PD&E, it can promote (a) identifying problems that have local value and import for daily living, (b) reducing programs that are perceived as being oppressive or exploitative by recipients, (c) better addressing social, health, and environmental inequities according to gender, race, ethnicity, and/or class that afflict many communities (Smith, 2005, 2008), and (d) including those with the everyday, local expertise that is essential to accurately shape programs so that they are culturally valid, useful, and sustainable (Jacobson & Rugeley, 2007).

The other side of the issue of ensuring local community involvement in PD&E is that the efforts need to yield programs that are consistent with evidence-based research and are able to generate evidence-based findings. This demand is a complex one. To be locally and generally valid is not easily attainable, and it often involves deciding on trade-offs along the way. Yet it is the aspiration.

Learning Exercise 2: Community Collaboration in Program Development

1. Explain the benefits and the challenges involved in trying to obtain community involvement in prevention program development.

   Benefits:

   Challenges:

2. What abilities do you think would be helpful in promoting community collaboration?

   Abilities needed:

   Self-assessment of my community collaboration abilities:

Cultural Relevance

When a program is parachuted down into a community, even a program that contains evidence of previous effectiveness (but with other populations in other settings), it is divorced from participation by *these* community members, and it also fails to take their unique needs and values and the culture of *this* community into consideration. "I know what's best for you" will not work with prevention programs.

By contrast, genuinely conducted community collaboration opens the possibility for accessing local needs, values, and culture. Developing positive working relationships between prevention program personnel and community members opens the potential for creating and implementing programs that are culturally valid and valued by the community. This point represents the essence of cultural relevance within prevention programs: *consistency between the programs themselves and how they were developed in relation to the beliefs, values, and preferred outcomes of community members* (Reese & Vera, 2007). Shaping prevention programs to attune them with cultural relevance is an important principle in the science and practice of prevention.

The Role of EBP

It is not enough, though, to create programs that work and satisfy local needs only. Of course, programs need to be effective and valuable locally to be sure, no argument at all. A further test is for them to be constructed in such a way as to be of value beyond the local environment, that is, to be generalizable to other populations and settings.

EBP is central to a local–general connection. It combines the concepts of research efficacy and clinical utility. See Book 6 for an expanded treatment of this topic.

Research efficacy, a *science* emphasis, refers to the strength of evidence indicating causal relationships between prevention programs and disorders or significant problems to be averted. Generalizability beyond the local population and setting to other similar populations and settings is associated with research efficacy.

Clinical utility is a *practice* emphasis. It draws from consensus about generalizing treatment programs consistent with research evidence and also considers the program's acceptability to clients, its feasibility, and its costs and benefits. These additional concerns hold consequences for local application.

EBP, therefore, combines the criteria of efficacy and utility. It is defined by the Institute of Medicine (2001, adapted from Sackett, Straus, Richardson, Rosenberg, & Hayes, 2000) as "the integration of best research evidence with clinical experience and patient values" (p. 147).

As extended to psychology, *Evidence-Based Practice in Psychology* (*EBPP*) expands the Institute of Medicine conception of EBP, giving fuller attention to client-related factors. The American Psychological Association Presidential Task Force on EBP (2006) defines EBPP as "the integration of the best available research with clinical expertise in the context of patient characteristics, culture, and preferences" (p. 273).

Notice the contextual emphasis inherent in the APA definition of EBPP, with particular consideration given to the *characteristics, culture, and preferences of clients*. This connection is salient for PD&E approaches that are community based and culturally relevant.

To more directly fit the prevention focus of this *Kit* and in this book, the clinically oriented language of EBPP needs to be changed a bit. So, for prevention programs, a parallel statement might read as the following:

> Evidence-Based Practice in *Prevention Programs* combines two sets of criteria of efficacy and utility yielding the integration of best research evidence with *prevention* experience and expertise in the context of *participant* characteristics, culture, preferences, values, and principles.

Counseling, prevention, and other psychological services are most likely to be effective when they anticipate or respond to the participant's unique context, which includes the following:

- Specific problems
- Strengths and goals
- Chronological age and developmental history
- Preferences, beliefs, interests, values, and worldviews
- Characteristics, personality, gender, ethnicity, race, social class
- The sociocultural and environmental context (APA, 2002; Norcross, 2002; Sue, Zane, & Young, 1994)

These contextual influences are linked through the professional judgment of the practitioner with the best research available. Research findings considered are not restricted to any one model. Rather, this research can be produced through multiple methods, including the following: (a) efficacy, effectiveness, cost–benefit, epidemiological, and treatment utilization; (b) quantitative and qualitative designs, as well as clinical observation; (c) experimental and natural settings; and (d) process and outcomes studies. Systematic reviews, meta-analyses, effect sizes, and both statistical and clinical evidence are typically relied on to identify the best available research (APA, 2002).

Search for EBP Models

A number of credible sources point to evidence-based programs. For instance, the Center for the Study and Prevention of Violence (2002–2004) contains a searchable set of violence prevention programs that have been judged as effective. In its *Blueprints for Violence Prevention* project, 11 prevention and intervention "Blueprints" programs are identified that meet a strict scientific standard of program effectiveness. These 11 programs have been found to be effective in reducing adolescent violent crime, aggression, delinquency, and substance abuse. Another 18 programs have been identified as "promising" programs. More than 600 programs have been reviewed, and the Center continues to look for programs that meet the selection criteria.

Blueprint programs can be examined for potential adoption. Sometimes, a program used elsewhere can fit well in a different location with a similar population. As pointed out, though, most likely adaptation will be needed to fit the program with the local community and its members because ecologies differ across settings. A critical concern always relates to the program's cultural relevance. How will it fit the local community? What adjustments of "noncore" factors could be made to improve its cultural relevance without cutting into the "meat" of the program? How can local ecological assessment information be used to assist in that goal?

A community-based, collaborative, and culturally relevant PD&E approach to prevention seeks to yield programs that are useful in the local community and that can be generalized to the scientific community as well. Including efficacy-based practices that are culturally relevant is a key aspect of such an approach.

Summary

PD&E is a subset of the fields of program evaluation and evaluation research. In this chapter, you read about different PD&E approaches that have emerged and that can be very helpful in practice. These include *the Logic Model, PROCEED–PRECEDE, Utilization-Focused Evaluation, CIPP, Differential Social Program Evaluation*, the *Effectiveness-Based* Approach, the *HIP Pocket Guide*, the *CASEL* format, the *Student Service Program Development Model*, and the *Transformative Research and Evaluation* approach. In addition, the role of community, collaboration, cultural relevance, and EBP were considered in relation to PD&E in prevention approaches, including adaptations in terminology meant to better fit prevention.

3

Defining Program Development and Evaluation

I n all books within this *Kit*, we want to emphasize concrete, practical, and research-guided applications for improving preventive practice, while also providing supportive theoretical and conceptual issues. Indeed, concerning prevention in mental health, two of the most frequently asked questions put to me over the decades still are these: (1) "The idea of prevention seems attractive but I get confused about it—what is prevention?" and (2) "I think I understand prevention pretty well—but how do you *do* prevention?" This chapter will attempt to answer the first of these questions: "What is prevention?" The following chapter will address the issue of doing prevention.

In this chapter, PD&E is defined generically, without giving particular attention to PD&E steps or to prevention (*Editors' note:* See Book 8 in this Kit for program development and evaluation within Public Policy and Analysis). At this point, we can be content with developing a basic understanding of the PD&E process. In addition, seven general evaluation criteria that are important for both program development and for program evaluation are presented.

Defining PD&E

PD&E refers to "a dynamic procedure containing a sequenced and coordinated set of steps that harnesses and directs resources and forces toward desired and testable goal accomplishment" (Conyne, 2010). This definition needs some elaboration. PD&E is a

> *Dynamic procedure containing a sequenced set of steps.* PD&E is a procedure consisting of a systematic series of steps that are followed in order to produce a program or intervention that can reach established goals. It is dynamic, subject to appropriate adaptation that is consistent with the ebb and flow that characterize any human system.

Harnesses and directs resources and forces. This dynamic procedure focuses on heightening forces that already may be present in a setting and/or on introducing innovation within the setting. In either case, the procedure needs to include processes of collaboration and participation, and be evidence-based. (p. 76)

Taking advantage of already existing forces and settings provides one PD&E approach. Examples of such naturally occurring settings and conditions (i.e., not initiated by the prevention program) include soup kitchens, nursing homes, schools, the natural resilience of a population, informal or indigenous sources of help in the community, places of worship, and neighborhood parks and the everyday activities that take place in them. Prevention programs can be developed around ongoing activities that organically nurture, challenge, and support people in the setting, harnessing these salutary interactions to reach designated goals. By doing so, social competency is facilitated from existing dynamics (Gullotta & Bloom, 2003), rather than being introduced anew from the outside. This approach maximizes the important values of authenticity and participant involvement (Goldston et al., 2008).

In a second approach, programs are created or concocted where none existed. This is more frequent and typifies how PD&E generally is understood and practiced. Here, program planners move through a series of sequenced steps to introduce a planned intervention within a setting in order to benefit participants.

Toward desired and testable goal accomplishment. Programs are intended to resolve problems and reach goals. Prevention programs are intended to strengthen people in settings and to reduce the incidence of identified disorders. Programs, as we have pointed out, are the means to the end, the engine that drives the effort toward goal accomplishment. The program plan is constructed to allow for evaluation of the implementation process against the intended plan (termed process or formative evaluation), of outcomes (termed outcome or summative evaluation) and their impact, and the timely dissemination of results in usable formats to appropriate audiences. (Conyne, 2010, p. 76)

General Evaluation Criteria in PD&E

Program evaluation is a systematic process that is conducted to obtain information on a program's activities, its effectiveness, and its impact so that the program can be improved and its goals accomplished (Perales, 2010). This systematic process includes attending to certain evaluation criteria. Programs need to be constructed with sensitivity, given to certain general evaluation criteria. These criteria also provide an important means for evaluating the processes and outcomes of programs. These general evaluation criteria are the following:

A: Adequacy

A: Appropriateness

E: Effectiveness

E: Efficiency

S: Side effects (Craig, 1978)

Each criterion contains important questions to ask when determining if any program has been delivered properly and has been beneficial. The same criteria are among those that can be asked—and should be asked—not only at the end of a program but also at its beginning and all the way through its application.

While being core considerations in PD&E, contemporary understanding suggests that these five criteria may not tell the whole story. As research and practice have evolved, including considerations drawn from an ecological orientation (e.g., Bronfenbrenner, 1979; Conyne & Cook, 2004; Conyne, Crowell, & Newmeyer, 2008; Kelly & Hess, 1987), two additional criteria add substance: *Context* and *Sustainability*.

Let's take a closer look at these seven criteria for PD&E. For an expanded discussion, see Craig (1978) and Conyne (2010).

Context

Context is a "surrounds" criterion. It refers to the situation surrounding and influencing a population and setting of interest. Contextual variables might include culture, values, history, economics, geography, and weather—salient properties and processes that surround and influence the population. In a sense, you can think of context as being analogous to the water surrounding a fish.

For instance, neighborhoods in the same city can vary considerably in relation to their local contexts. One may be noted for its high quality of life, safety, and abundance of resources, while another across town might be plagued by high crime, high unemployment, and few resources. Going to school in one place or another, therefore, even at the same grade levels can be quite different experiences due, to a large extent, to context.

The above discussion of contextual influences addressed proximal (near by, close) ones, which tend to exert a continual press. Contextual influences also can be distal (far away), arising from national or international sources. A nation's monetary structure, results of a political election, the threat of military attack, and the predominant jet stream off the western coast are all examples of distal forces. Economic conditions continue to rank as the number one concern among U.S. citizens. Mortgage foreclosures, zooming gasoline prices, the falling dollar, a lagging housing industry, and a stubbornly high unemployment rate exert their pernicious effects on millions of people in the United States and around the world. These macrolevel economic conditions add to the context of people's lives.

Therefore, PD&E approaches need to assess both proximal and distal contextual influences. All other evaluative criteria are moderated by their impact.

Adequacy

Adequacy is a strength–weakness criterion. A program or intervention needs to contain sufficient dosage and potency to produce the desired effect. The "Goldilocks Rule" applies, so that neither too much nor too little of a program is needed, but it needs to be "just about right." In one example (Lum, 2011) of applying the criterion of adequacy, the most recent tabulation (2008–2009) of the ratio of school counselors to students in U.S. public schools is 457:1; and the recommended maximum average ratio by the American Counseling Association is 250:1. This large negative discrepancy suggests that, except for the five states where the recommended ratio is met, the school counselor–to-student ratio is inadequate in 45 of our states. As a result, there are just not enough school counselors available to assist in promoting student well-being and academic achievement, among other goals. In another example, a senior citizen program intended to improve physical balance and flexibility may be insufficient (too weak) if it fails to include attention to social support among participants. There must be "the right stuff" (Wolfe, 1979) to produce desired effects.

Appropriateness

Appropriateness is a right–wrong criterion. But a prevention program needs more than the right stuff. It also must be presented in the "right way," that is—in a way that matches with the values and culture of the population. What makes a program successful for one population may not be suited for another one. Or it may take some time and adaptation for the program to become acceptable.

A story in the morning news (Martin, 2011) caught my eye. It was about the concern of many school districts with students wearing breast cancer awareness bracelets containing the insignia, "I (heart symbol) boobies!" Having been banned in some districts, the matter currently is before a federal court in Pennsylvania. Concerned school district personnel report wanting to support breast cancer awareness messages but disapprove of the "double entendre" they see involved with this particular message. For those school districts, the style of the message—which might score high on the evaluation criterion of effectiveness—conflicts with their culture and may conflict with their existing policies, and is deemed inappropriate.

Mental health treatment may be accepted and even desired by large numbers of citizens in upscale and educated urban populations and yet be largely distrusted and unwelcomed in some rural communities whose citizens live in poverty and without the benefits of advanced education. This is not an argument for withholding mental health services from these rural settings but, rather, for recognizing that such services will need to be uniquely matched to the existing cultural and ecological situation.

Cultural relevance is a key appropriateness concern. "Cultural invasion" needs to be avoided, where outside experts introduce programs—even when evidence-based—without the consent and participation of local people and when they are at odds with the local culture, history, and values. Ignoring this point virtually guarantees that a program will fail.

Appropriateness of an intervention depends on matching it closely with characteristics of the population (and setting) for whom it is intended. Advancements in multicultural counseling and diversity (e.g., American Psychological Association, 2002; Association for Specialists in Group Work, 1998; Sue, Arredondo, & McDavis, 1992), in best practice guidelines for prevention (Hage et al., 2007), and in culturally relevant prevention (Reese & Vera, 2007) have raised awareness about the need for exercising appropriateness in interventions and programs and have provided guidelines to improve that practice.

Effectiveness

Effectiveness is a successful–not successful criterion. As mentioned above, two types of program evaluation are conducted to determine success: (1) process or formative evaluation, which is concerned with how a program is being delivered in relation to its plan; and (2) outcome or summative evaluation, which is determined by evaluating program results in relation to program and individual goals that shaped the program's delivery.

As we have seen in earlier discussions of evidence-based programs, rigorous research and evaluation of program outcomes is considered the "gold standard." Thus, it is treated as a kind of "super criterion," in relation to the others.

Effectiveness research seeks to answer the fundamental question: "Did the program work?" That is, at the conclusion of the program were its goals accomplished? If so, to what degree was it accomplished? An even more sophisticated effectiveness question is, "Compared to no program or to an alternative one, did this program produce a positive effect that is appreciably or statistically significant?" Gradually, effective programs and practices can be identified for replication and adaptation elsewhere.

Kazdin (2008) recognizes the renewed emphasis within psychology and other disciplines to better link effective treatments with effective practice—not only to develop a stronger connection—but also to enhance knowledge and improve care. Science is much more than significance levels, effect sizes, and randomization. While adherence to scientific methodologies is important, doing so sometimes is an aspirational quest, given real-world challenges (Conyne, 2004). Scientific methodologies need to be conducted, and perhaps modified, to fit the context and be responsive to changing conditions that are endemic to any community-based project (Vera, 2008; Vera et al., 2007).

Efficiency

Efficiency is a cost–value criterion. Following an expression of President Harry Truman, efficiency has been described as yielding "the biggest bang for the buck." Efficiency easily wins the equivalent of the Olympic "silver medal" due to the importance of value and cost-effectiveness. Here's but one example: Every $1.00 invested in work site wellness programs produces savings of $15.60 in reduced absenteeism (Aldana, Merrill, Price, Hardy, & Hager, 2005). Now that's efficient!

A program can be effective but not efficient. How is that so? I have used this illustration before (Conyne, 2010), where I asked readers to imagine two automobiles, each of which runs well and are of similar size and weight. Assume also that these autos can be driven between two points at the same rate of speed. However, one costs $60,000 and gets 18 miles of gas to the gallon. The other costs $14,000 and gets 26 miles to the gallon. The first burns premium fuel, while the second uses regular (to make the example even more stark, imagine the second car as a hybrid or an electric car). Each automobile moves people to their destinations effectively but efficiency clearly favors the second vehicle. The cars may not be equivalent in terms of attractiveness or perceived status, although perceptions of these attributes can change over time, and they may or may not matter to the driver. In any case, in terms of efficiency, the greater bang for the buck goes to Car 2.

Prevention programs contain a kind of built-in efficiency, which is one of their significant attractions. They are introduced early, before dysfunction or a particular state of unhealthiness has been established within persons. A program to assist those recently unemployed in finding new work is conducted, also, with the intention of averting depression, a mental health disorder that is very costly; the National Institutes of Mental Health estimates that $23 billion workdays are lost each year due to depression. In a simulated intervention based on many studies, researchers (Wang et al., 2006) reported that providing a minimal level of enhanced care in addressing the depression of employees would produce a cumulative savings to employers of $2,898 per 1,000 workers over 5 years by reducing the absenteeism and turnover costs of employees. In another example of efficiency (Paul, 2011), a short, 7-item depression screen administered to students going to university health centers for a physical complaint or ailment identified one fifth to one quarter as depressed, with 2% to 3% of them considering suicide. Effective screening measures are one highly endorsed method for identifying candidates for prevention programs. Programs provided early in or prior to depression can be expected to yield even greater cost-effectiveness.

Let's look at reported benefits and costs for three "model" research-based youth prevention programs (Washington State Institute for Public Policy, 2004). These figures show the benefit per dollar of cost:

Functional Family Therapy, addressing crime reduction $13.25

Life Skills Training, addressing drug reduction $25.61

Project Toward No Drug Abuse, addressing drug reduction $55.84

These programs show benefits over costs at multiples of 13, 26, and 56, respectively. Those numbers certainly show a very large "bang for the buck!" As well, in these cases, efficiency gains are accompanied by effectiveness, too, as the programs are proven stars at accomplishing their preventive goals.

Considerations of efficiency are always important with programs in mental health and education because the available resource base generally is small. Certainly, that condition applies to prevention programs also. All of these programs must be lean and parsimonious in terms of resources needed.

Indeed, efficiency assumes even more importance in times of scarcity, where resources are few and competition for them is high. Budgets in health care and education are always restricted, but during economic downturns they become particularly squeezed, in fact, often being among the first to be reduced. Too often, when under financial duress, school districts cut school counselors (and the arts), cities tend to excise funding for school nurses and health clinics, and businesses downsize human resources departments and wellness programs (if they exist).

Finding ways to "do more with less," a frequently expressed phrase today and over the past decade or so, demands close attention to questions of efficiency when designing and delivering quality programs. All things considered, efficiencies can be found when designing programs around activities and events endemic to a setting and by keeping imported resources to a minimum.

Side Effects

Side effects are an "oops!" criterion. Program planners keep "main effects" in mind. What are the goals? How will we reach those goals? Were we successful in reaching those goals? However, as scientists and the public both have learned, unintended effects—which can be positive as well as negative—always attend planned interventions.

Consider the baggage fees imposed by most airlines in their times of economic travail. This is really easy money. For instance, consider this personal case. My wife and I are about to fly on a ski vacation. We own ski equipment, and typically, we check it as baggage when we fly to ski. Better think again these days. To check skis on the airline we are flying would cost each of us $175 for each leg of the trip, or a total of $700. This is an example of an unintended negative side effect that plunders the flier, makes richer the airlines and the ski equipment rental agencies located at ski resorts, but may decrease the sales of ski equipment by ski stores that are located far away from those ski resorts.

Side effects in counseling are common. How clients respond and react to counseling interventions cannot always be predicted. A group member who learns in group how to become more assertive may find that her boss is not only surprised but is displeased about this new behavior and fires her. Including mentoring in a prevention program sometimes results in the mentor gaining at least as much as and sometimes more than the mentee, a phenomenon known as the "helper-therapy principle" (Riessman, 1965). The placebo effect, a phenomenon in research or in treatment where a participant's beliefs (positive or negative) about the outcome can significantly affect the outcome itself without any other intervention, can exert a powerful side effect.

In general, side effects are everywhere. The idea is to anticipate them better in planning programs. Unintended side effects can be reduced through vigilance during the planning process, by asking questions such as the following: What might happen that we haven't considered? What could go wrong that we haven't thought of yet? What might we be able to take advantage of, if it occurs?

Sustainability

Sustainability is a "last–fade" criterion. Program effects, when found, are subject to deterioration. Everyone knows about the high failure rate of maintaining New Year's resolutions. The gyms are crowded in early January, but attendance dwindles as the calendar pages turn. Maintaining active listening skills, avoiding eating snacks while watching a favorite television program, or practicing newly learned meditation skills daily can all dissipate without focused and continued attention to sustaining them.

Program effects are difficult to maintain over a long stretch due to the tendency of an effect to wither without the continued program and in the face of changing personal and environmental conditions over time. Recognizing this tendency, program components need to be designed for sustainability for their potential to promote the possibility that impacts will be maintained over time.

As well, parallel evaluation procedures need to be sensitive to measuring postprogram effects. Booster sessions have been found to be useful in promoting sustainability, matched by accompanying evaluation points. Moreover, programs that have been created by or in collaboration with community members hold a greater likelihood of sustainability due to the direct stake of participants in the process and to their firsthand observation of positive changes (Goldston et al., 2008).

The general evaluation criteria just discussed are important to include in any PD&E plan to assist with designing the plan well and with guiding process and outcome evaluations. Let's refresh your understanding of them.

Learning Exercise 3: True–False

1. Program development and evaluation emerges from the broad fields of program evaluation and evaluation research.

2. Involving participants in all phases of program development and evaluation is desirable and unrealistic.

3. At its roots, PD&E depends on a technical process.

4. Attention to community, collaboration, and cultural relevance are completely foreign to PD&E models.

5. Evidence-based approaches do not apply to prevention program development and evaluation.

Learning Exercise 4: Mix and Match

Try matching the seven evaluative criteria with their brief descriptors.

INSTRUCTIONS: Match criterion letters with the correct descriptor number and place in the blank.

Criteria Brief Descriptor Correct Match (letter–number)

(a)	Context	(1) Cost–Value _____	
(b)	Adequacy	(2) Last–Fade _____	
(c)	Appropriateness	(3) Successful–Unsuccessful _____	
(d)	Effectiveness	(4) Surrounds _____	
(e)	Efficiency	(5) Ooops! _____	
(f)	Side effects	(6) Strength–Weakness _____	
(g)	Sustainability	(7) Right–Wrong _____	

Summary

This chapter focuses on presenting fundamental definitions. PD&E is defined as "*a dynamic procedure containing a sequenced and coordinated set of steps that harnesses and directs resources and forces toward desired and testable goal accomplishment*" (Conyne, 2010, p. 76). Seven general evaluation criteria are then defined that are important for both program development and for program evaluation: context, appropriateness, adequacy, effectiveness, efficiency, side effects, and sustainability.

4 Practical Steps for Applying Program Development and Evaluation in Prevention

With this chapter, we focus on the role of PD&E in *doing* prevention and determining its worth. As I pointed out, this is one of the main questions asked by practitioners who are interested in prevention but don't know where and how to start.

Essentially, procedures for conducting prevention hinge on the PD&E process. As Perales (2010) put it, "Evaluation is a necessary element for documenting the success of prevention efforts" (p. 206).

As you have read, programs are how prevention goals are pursued. Program development steps guide the creation of such programs, and program evaluation is conducted to keep programs on course (process evaluation) and to determine if they were beneficial and, if so, how effective and in what ways (outcome evaluation).

The PD&E process needs to accommodate three central conditions:

1. To appropriately blend evidence-based findings with local conditions

2. To be guided by a sequenced set of steps that leads from understanding what is missing and needed through development and implementation of the prevention product

3. To evaluate the program's process as it is being conducted and its preventive effects

As I wish to point out once again, special care needs to be taken in the PD&E process to involve setting participants throughout and to avoid what is an all-too-common tendency to insert and manage programs from the "top-down," providing what planners think might be best based on research or on their own experience and expertise. Equal care needs to be given to program alterations that better fit community conditions, while not stripping the program of its change-producing essence.

A 10-step, sequenced PD&E plan is presented and discussed for the remainder of this chapter. These steps are arranged within three hierarchical PD&E cycles:

A. Plan (five steps)
B. Implement (two steps)
C. Effects (three steps)

In full array, the steps are (see Conyne, 2010, for more detail for each step, especially Steps 1 and 3 of Planning) as follows.

The 10-Step PD&E in Prevention Model

A. Plan the program

1. *Lay the groundwork for community, collaboration, and cultural relevance.*

2. *Analyze local context and conduct professional literature review.*

3. *Create problem statement.*

4. *Develop preventive goals, objectives, strategies, and evaluation.*

5. *Obtain inputs and resources.*

B. Implement, including process evaluation

6. *Implement program plan with participants through strategies comprising sequenced and coordinated activities, tasks, responsibilities, resources, and timelines.*

7. *Examine process evaluation data to generate feedback.*

C. Effects: evaluate outputs

8. *Examine outcome evaluation data to determine outcomes.*

9. *Identify impacts, incidence reduction.*

10. *Disseminate results.*

Each of the PD&E steps is discussed in the following section. But before proceeding, complete the next Learning Exercise.

Learning Exercise 5: Apply Your Personal Prevention Program

Choose something you are interested in or concerned about (e.g., the problem of dental cavities or that of too many lonely weekends) to work on as you read the steps of this PD&E model. The steps are presented below for easy guidance and for note taking.

Apply the steps to your personal example in a 5-page outline, organized by the 10 steps of the PD&E in Prevention Model.

Plan

Step 1: Lay the groundwork for community, collaboration, and cultural relevance. *Conduct group work, team building, and collaboration processes to create and maintain an effective planning unit that represents important constituent groups.*

Prevention programs and their development and evaluation are products of people. They emerge from the interactions of people with each other and with data and things over time. PD&E is a process for organizing and guiding these efforts. Its effectiveness depends on many factors, not the least of which is the groundwork that is laid in early developmental stages. This groundwork involves the creation and maintenance of collaborative, community-based processes that fit the culture of the population and the setting in which the prevention program is to be implemented.

I will focus this step on aspects of team development, which is one of the central ingredients of laying the groundwork. In other sections of this book, attention is given to the importance of collaboration and attending to cultural sensitivities. Refer to Conyne (2010) for more expansive discussion of all these points.

Establish and Maintain a Team. Developing a program requires many resources, including a base of support or a team. Acting as a solo agent virtually guarantees failure. The tasks are too complex. They demand experience and expertise that no one person possesses.

An example from the animal world clearly illustrates the value of a team, where a huge alligator is outwitted and bedazzled by a number of far smaller otters working together as a team, allowing all individuals to survive and to live for another day (see *"A Group of Brave Otters vs. an Alligator,"* 2011). A team whose members learn how to function collaboratively can help develop and guide initiatives and obtain necessary support.

Interpersonal Skills. Accomplishing this first step successfully takes skill and continual attention. Actually, the process begins with self-assessment of your attitude and skills. To form a base of support, or a team, requires interest and skills in working with others. In fact, the entire prevention planning process depends strongly on possessing a positive interpersonal attitude and skills. Great ideas need to be complemented by equally great attitude and skills.

The crux of the matter for putting a team together is that interpersonal sensitivity and ability are forces that drive accomplishment along with commitment to the prevention process. An important question to address is "How interpersonally adept are you?

Learning Exercise 6: Assess Your Interpersonal Skills

This learning exercise provides you with an opportunity to self-assess your existing interpersonal skills.

*Respond to the first five questions below. Circle the number that best captures your **general** assessment, where: "1" = never to "5" = always, and then briefly explain them:*

1. I enjoy being with other people. 1 2 3 4 5

2. I am effective when working with others on tasks. 1 2 3 4 5

3. Others tend to like spending time with me. 1 2 3 4 5

4. I like working with people in groups. 1 2 3 4 5

5. My skills are sufficient for working with others. 1 2 3 4 5

In questions 6 and 7, jot down your thoughts:

6. In completing this exercise, I learned that my interpersonal strengths seem to be the following:

7. In completing this exercise, I learned I might need to improve the following:

Obtain Sanction. At an early point, it is necessary to garner support for forming and maintaining a prevention team. Being a staff member of a mental health or educational agency affords a natural opportunity to acquire the legitimacy that is required. Of course, if one already occupies a staff role connected with prevention (e.g., Coordinator of Prevention Services), or with group interventions (e.g., Coordinator of Group Services), the legitimacy usually is conferred. Otherwise, it has to be created. In such cases, interpersonal skills need to be enhanced with organizational skills to advocate persuasively for formation of a prevention team.

Team Development. Once a team is formed, it is necessary to develop it. What makes a set of people a team is that they come to develop a sense of mutuality and interdependence. They join in a common purpose that defines their existence as a team and they begin to accept that they are all part of the unit where each one is an important and meaningful contributor. The sense of cohesion that emerges in a well-functioning team is essential for maintaining the team over the long haul and for stimulating productivity (Fujishin, 2001).

Team Maintenance. After the team is developed, it needs to be maintained and sustained. This requires the team leader and its members to attend to the quality of team functioning (process) and to its success (outcome). Periodic review of how the team is doing can be very helpful for keeping progress on track.

The keys are to develop a culture where team members are interested in considering and responding to these kinds of questions and will be likely to follow up on the feedback that emerges when they examine them. Feedback that results from discussion of items such as these is used to identify next steps. These include (a) what is working and should be continued and (b) what is not working so well and should be improved.

Team Facilitation. Of course, it takes good team facilitation to produce a well-functioning team that moves forward positively over time. This means someone who is competent in group process and group leadership. Too frequently, leaders of task groups, teams, and committees are untrained in group work and have little or no supervised experience. It is no surprise, then, that their teams may not fare well.

Training and supervised experience in group work helps a team leader to be able to think and behave in relation to the team as a whole, its intermember relationships, and with respect to individual members as the team seeks to meet its tasks and responsibilities (Conyne, 1989; Conyne et al., 2008; Conyne, Rapin, & Rand, 1997; Hulse-Killacky, Killacky, & Donigian, 2001; Schwarz, 2002). Team facilitators need to be able to balance content and process dimensions that are sensitive to its various developmental stages. Hulse-Killacky et al. (2001) identified these task group stages quite simply as warm up, action, and closure. As well, facilitators need to help the team function well within the demands and resources of its external environment allowing problem-solving and group processes to be mobilized, yielding prevention programs that work (Conyne et al., 1997).

Step 2: Analyze local context and conduct professional literature review. *Examine local documents and records; interview key informants; observe; assess needs, assets, and environment; review relevant professional literature.*

As Professor Henry Hill, who was very adept at taking advantage of/conning new communities he entered, maintained in *The Music Man* (Wilson, 1950), *"Ya gotta know the territory!"* Conyne and Clack (1981) drew from this quote in their *Environmental Assessment and Design* book to lend an ordinary perspective to local assessment, not to usurp people as the otherwise delightful Professor Hill did but to learn about them and their environment so that helpful, useful, and effective prevention programs might be introduced. As we said then,

> One comes to know the territory by sharpening one's senses and getting to know the lay of the land and the people who live there. Actually, these are still basic methods that characterize many environmental classification approaches. (p. 21)

Local data can be gathered through a variety of means. The above quote addressed observation of a setting and how people behave in it. A sampling of other potential sources for local data gathering include participant observation, which involves both participating actively in an environment and observing its dynamics at the same time; reviewing published documents such as newspapers and newsletters; examining fliers posted on kiosks, car windshields, and in other public places; accessing public records available through the local levels of government; researching the range of local (and, of course, beyond) information available at the library; noting events covered by local radio and television news programs; and in today's world, being aware of postings and ongoing interactions at various locations on the Internet.

As well, local data can be generated through active data collection techniques. Interviews, focus groups, surveys, and questionnaires all exemplify the variety of active means that exist for this purpose.

Let's say that the collecting of local information indicated that high rates of school absenteeism and attrition and low graduation rates exist in the public schools. What is the related professional literature on this general topic? What studies have been reported? Are there hypotheses or even theories about school attendance and related negative outcomes? Have causal or contributing factors been identified? What populations seem most at risk locally, nationally, and globally? Is any of it preventable? Are there any preventive approaches that have been shown to work? How have these been developed? What results have been shown?

It is helpful when tackling complex tasks, such as a professional literature review, for team members to agree to handle certain tasks. For instance, one person might explore the Internet, another might investigate the local university library. Or if subtopics have been identified already, they could be assigned to different team members: dropping out, school engagement, teacher–student relationships, parent involvement, community support, and other issues—whatever might have been identified in the community assessment.

Once assignments are differentiated, then what is produced needs to be coordinated. Indeed, coordinating and integrating team member functioning is a general and ongoing challenge. In the case of a differentiated literature review, obtaining and pulling together information into a usable and meaningful product can be taxing, or rewarding, depending on how it goes. If you've ever worked on a team-based project, you can relate to this matter. It is helpful to have a system to follow. In Conyne (2010), I discussed one such system called "problem-based learning," which has shown to be helpful.

Step 3: Create the problem statement. *Identify clearly, concisely, and concretely what is missing and what is not working in the situation faced. For prevention programs, define the problem in terms of incidence reduction (see Albee, 1982; Conyne, 2010; for a detailed discussion of this procedure).*

Determine the Problem in General Terms. *What is a problem?* Adapted from a classic definition by Craig (1978), a problem generally can be understood as a situation or condition of people or an environment that is considered to be undesirable. Unless something is done to change that situation or condition, the problem will continue to exist in the future. Moreover, in prevention, the key is to stop problem onset or to reduce the rate of onset.

Analyzing a problem aids in understanding it and in how to address it. Some important analytical questions include (Craig, 1978; Kettner et al., 2008) the following:

- What is the nature of the situation or condition?
- How do people experience this problem?
- Whose problem is it?
- What seem to be its causes?
- What is the scope of the problem?
- How does the situation or condition fit with local values?
- Are ethnic, gender, class, or other issues of diversity involved?
- What may happen if nothing is done?

Mental health and education problems inhibit successful and satisfying functioning. These can run a broad gamut ranging across psychological and emotional disturbances (e.g., depression), negative lifestyles involving repetitive bad choices, and dysfunctional behaviors such as missing school or violence against self or others.

Define the Problem in Incidence Reduction Terms. In prevention, the goal is to stop or minimize undesirable, hurtful problems from emerging in the first place—or as quickly as possible, once it has progressed—through environmental change and personal change programmatic efforts. This is incidence reduction. In short, the relevant questions for incidence reduction are (Romano & Hage, 2000) as follows:

- Has problem onset been stopped?

This is the sine qua non of primary prevention and incidence reduction. For instance, did the prevention program stop the emergence of overweight and obesity in new cases of the population? Did the school attrition prevention program stop new dropouts from occurring?

- Has its rate of development been slowed, delayed, or reduced?

As an alternative to stopping an undesirable behavior or circumstance, which often is difficult and impossible to achieve, was it slowed, delayed, or reduced? Compared with past evidence for obesity in a population, were the numbers of new cases, or their rate of development, reduced?

- Have strengths that promote and sustain emotional and physical well-being been created?

In a midrange incidence reduction strategy, prevention programs should help participants develop new knowledge, attitudes, and skills that can serve to inoculate them from future threats. Have program participants learned how to eat more nutritiously, are they beginning to put into effect other positive lifestyle behaviors, such as appropriate levels of physical exercise, or developing stronger social bonds?

- Have environmental changes been put into place to more fully support positive behavior change?

In another midrange incidence reduction strategy, prevention programs should aim to intentionally modify existing negative environmental conditions, through social justice and other system change approaches, to provide more equitable and healthier options. For instance, does a school cafeteria now offer a healthier selection of food choices for students, or has a new policy to prevent sexual harassment been adopted?

- Are problem conditions prevented indirectly?

Being able to show reductions in a currently existing problem condition within a population, such as in the number of those presently bullying other students in a high school class, is a remedial (or tertiary prevention) treatment intervention and by itself would not be classified as early-stage prevention. Yet direct effects such as this one can radiate to exert truly preventive impact in related areas. In this example of bullying, preventive effects might be realized through a generally improved school climate of increased tolerance, acceptance, and respect that might contribute to a safer and more supportive school environment for future students.

Step 4: Develop preventive goals, objectives, strategies, and evaluation: Preventive goals are defined (universal, selective, or indicated) and goals and objectives (specific, performance-based, attainable, measurable, and observable) are stated. *The goals and objectives give focus to program development and implementation and serve to organize program evaluation. (Note: Program strategies and evaluation will be considered in Steps 6 to 10, below.)*

Program objectives make the general program goals more specific and concrete. A goal statement represents the final destination, the end point. Objectives, in a sense, are smaller goals that, when combined, form a goal. A sports' analogy might help clarify the difference between a goal and an objective. In baseball, a goal is to win by scoring more runs than the opponent. That's a general and necessary goal. To accomplish this goal, a range of objectives must be met, including getting hits, making plays on defense, avoiding errors, advancing the runner, driving in base runners, holding the opponent to the lowest outputs (runs, but also batting average, runs batted in, etc.), producing the highest outputs possible, and more. In a prevention program, a goal might be to increase the resiliency of sixth-grade students of Grant School, while some objectives might include increasing problem-solving skills by 75% and decreasing reported stressors by 25%.

Arguably, it is important and necessary to develop goals and objectives in life. In program development and evaluation, there is little argument that this step is necessary.

The relation between an objective and a problem is inverted. That is, an objective essentially is a problem tilted upside down. Again, an example might help. If the problem is that there are way too many overweight children and adults in Clovedale, an objective might be for program participants there to reduce their weight by 5% on average in 6 weeks. So, where the problem identifies a situation or condition that is *undesirable*, an objective converts the deficit into a statement of *desirability* that also has the potential to be *changed* and *measured*.

Objectives stem from goals, which set an overall direction for action. Objectives are more precise than goals. The acronym, "SPAMO," refers to conditions that, if enacted, can help define some of this precision. According to SPAMO, an objective needs to be as follows:

S: Specific and concrete, not vague, general, or ephemeral

P: Pertinent and relevant, connected to the program, not random or unattached

A: Attainable and achievable, feasible, real world not idealistic pie in the sky

M: Measurable and assessable, subject to being tested and examined

O: Objective and observable, behavioral, not subjective and internal

Objectives also need to be clearly and concretely written so that anyone who reads them will be able to understand them. It is helpful, as well, to tie criteria for success to objectives that can be used to evaluate whether the program and participants were able to achieve what was set out for them.

Step 5: Obtain inputs and resources. *Inputs and resources are tangible and intangible, both taken in from the external environment and found within program participants. These "raw materials" need to be managed and transformed through program activities into products.*

Inputs and resources can be thought of as raw materials needing to be transformed through activities into products. These raw materials are both tangible and intangible. On the tangible side, some common examples include people, skills, technology, money, space, and equipment. But intangible aspects can be as, and sometimes even more, critical. The interest, motivation, positive attitudes, and perseverance of people involved with a project contribute very strongly to its eventual success or failure. These inputs and resources need to be organized within a program development plan to support the creation of activities that will lead to goal accomplishment.

Back to our baseball example, it is no doubt more possible to win more games if a team comprises highly talented and skilled players. The same could be said of a symphony or any other ensemble-based effort. But, in addition to their talents, members also need to be motivated, possess positive attitudes, and care for the collective more than for their own individual advancement. Coaching and teaching strategies contribute substantially in helping team members transform their individual raw materials into productive and interdependent team functioning, whether on the ball field or in the performance hall. Developing a prevention program is no different.

Inputs and resources can be evaluated by their appropriateness, adequacy, feasibility, and sustainability. Do the inputs and resources match the cultural values, mores, principles, and history of the people and setting? That is, are they appropriate for the local community? Are the inputs and resources available adequate for goal accomplishment, or are more or different kinds of resources needed? Is it feasible that these inputs and resources will allow the program to continue over time, that is, to be sustained?

Implement, Including Process Evaluation

Steps 6 and 7: Implement program plan with participants and establish process monitoring and feedback mechanism. *Apply the plan's strategies, each of which comprises sequenced and coordinated activities, tasks, responsibilities, resources, and timelines that are tailored to participant groups; determine satisfaction of participants; conduct process evaluation involving fidelity with plan; monitor and analyze ongoing feedback; and make modifications as needed.*

Step 6 is defined as implementing the program plan with participants through strategies, which comprise sequenced and coordinated activities, tasks, responsibilities, resources, and timelines. In general, the charge in this step is to enumerate relationships among the targeted problem, goals, and objectives of the program and strategies to be followed in reaching those objectives. "Strategies," then, are the general means through which goals and objectives are intended to be met.

A *strategy* comprises several linked components: (a) *activities*, which are its basic building blocks; (b) *tasks* (which can be thought of as miniactivities) to be accomplished within each activity; (c) *responsibilities* to be fulfilled in discharging each task, which tie what needs to be done to specific people or groups; (d) *resources*, including tangible (e.g., money) and intangible assets (e.g., competencies) required to fulfill the tasks; and (e) *timelines* for completing the strategies, activities, and tasks. By following this schema, any strategy is broken down into concrete parts and processes that specify and clarify proper implementation.

Step 7 is defined as examining process evaluation data to generate feedback. The duty in this step is to design and implement monitoring and feedback procedures to provide program planners with the information needed to keep track of how the program is actually being implemented in relation to the original plan for it—and then to be able to make any necessary modifications to keep it, or to get it, on course.

As you can see, Step 6 allows program planning and implementation to become increasingly more targeted and specific. One of the challenges that always nags program development and evaluation is that the complexity and number of people involved in programs promote blurred responsibility and confusion, a perfect instance of "the left hand not knowing what the right hand is doing." The sequenced and coordinated process contained in Step 6 serves to clarify who-is-to-do-what-when. The process evaluation considerations contained in Step 7 permit monitoring of this plan, yielding data that can be used by planners to continually improve implementation.

The general program development and evaluation sequence within the program implementation stage follows:

Problem–Objectives–Strategies–Activities–Tasks–Responsibilities–Resources–Timelines–Process Evaluation

Example

In the example about school attrition sketched below, note how the objective emerges from the problem statement. The implementation plan in this illustration is that the objective will be met through four strategies, each one containing the elements of activity, task, responsibilities, resources, timeline, and evaluation. In reality, each strategy typically comprises more than one and perhaps several activities, each one containing tasks, responsibilities, resources, timelines, and evaluation. Refer to Craig (1978) and Conyne (2010) for a fuller depiction of these relationships, including schema (e.g., the Program Evaluation and Review Technique) for organizing the information.

Context: Six schools have been selected to participate in a "Healthy Schools" grant obtained recently by the university, in conjunction with the school district.

Problem statement: Too many students in the high schools involved with the Healthy Schools grant have low attendance, report disliking school, and fail to graduate.

Objective 1: To improve the attendance rate of next school year's entering freshmen class in one target school by 10% over previous figures (*Note:* the hypothesis is that improving attendance, if it can be maintained over time, will lead to improved positive connections of students with school and ultimately with enhanced opportunities for success, including graduation).

Strategy 1: Establish a baseline set of attendance data for the current freshman class against which to compare the attendance of the entering freshman class.

Sample activity: Create a research team to design, conduct, and report findings.

Sample task: Identify a process of selecting members for the research team.

Sample responsibilities: Specify whose responsibility it is to act on the results obtained.

Sample resources: Determine what technological resources will be needed to support the research process.

Sample timeline: Set the deadline for research results for 3 months from research team formation.

Sample process evaluation: Ask the research team to provide monthly updates of its progress and to provide a written report specifying attendance rate of the current freshman class by the due date.

Strategy 2: Determine satisfaction of all current freshmen with their high school experience.

Sample activity: Charge existing research team with coordinating this strategy.

Sample task: Review and select appropriate measures of student satisfaction.

Sample responsibilities: Determine whose responsibility it is to act on the results.

Sample resources: Acquire supportive finances for purchasing instrumentation and other data collection and analysis methods.

Sample timeline: Data analysis completed within 10 weeks.

Sample process evaluation: Design a method for determining if satisfaction data produced provides a clear baseline that could be used to compare against following the program's implementation.

Strategy 3: Develop a mentoring program aimed at positively connecting entering freshmen with their high school.

Sample activity: Identify evidence-based mentoring programs.

Sample task: Modify the selected program to best fit local circumstances while retaining core aspects of the program itself.

Sample responsibilities: Identify who will be responsible for the various aspects of the mentoring training program.

Sample resources: Obtain qualified trainers needed for the program.

Sample timeline: Design a schedule for completing each component of the mentoring training program and its final completion date.

Sample process evaluation: Design an ongoing feedback procedure to allow for continuous examination of the fidelity of the mentoring program's implementation in relation to the implementation plan for it (e.g., Is the number of planned training sessions occurring as planned?).

Strategy 4: Hire two school counselors and two school nurses to augment efforts to reduce absenteeism, improve academic and social behavior, and spearhead the drive toward improved graduation rates.

Sample activity: Create evidence-based rationale to support funding request.

Sample task: Conduct professional literature review to drive the rationale to be developed.

Sample responsibilities: Identify who will present completed rationale and funding request to whom.

Sample resources: Calculate costs and benefits for hiring the new staff.

Sample timeline: Determine when rationale will be completed and overall funding request submitted.

Sample process evaluation: Develop a monitoring plan for the counselors and nurses (if hired) to report their weekly activities and the number of contact hours they have with students, teachers, staff, and community members.

You can see how the planning process becomes ever more specific and concrete, progressing next to resources needed, timelines, and designation of responsibilities to persons or groups.

Effects: Evaluate Outcomes

Evaluation data need to be collected throughout the program. As mentioned under Implementation above, the program's processes are continually evaluated (process evaluation), providing ongoing feedback to inform decision making aimed at keeping the program on track. Program outcomes and impacts are evaluated at its end to determine if program goals were accomplished and if preventive effects were realized. Finally, program results need to be disseminated promptly and in ways that will communicate effectively with target audiences.

Program evaluation planning needs to be concerned with many issues, including maintaining sensitivity to the seven evaluation criteria we considered earlier: context, appropriateness, adequacy, effectiveness, efficiency, sustainability, and side effects. Perhaps foremost among these criteria is that of determining program effects through evaluating its outcomes and impacts. In addition, in the case of prevention programs, it is also important that evaluation consider incidence reduction.

In 1999, the Centers for Disease Control and Prevention published a framework for conducting program evaluation in public health, which has influenced other fields as well, including education and psychology. The five steps suggested in that document are similar to those already recommended in this book:

1. Engage stakeholders in the process.

2. Describe the program's history, evolution, and theory.

3. Focus the evaluation plan, assess feasibility, and prioritize.

4. Gather data to answer evaluation questions.

5. Analyze data and report findings.

Of particular interest are what the Center termed *Standards* for conducting good evaluations of programs. The standards, again very similar to the evaluation criteria we have considered, address the following:

(a) *Utility:* Will the evaluation yield information that is timely and is geared to specific audiences?
(b) *Feasibility:* Can the evaluation's design be conducted realistically, given circumstances of time, resources, and expertise?
(c) *Propriety:* Are the evaluation design and processes appropriate for the population and the setting, do they protect individual welfare, do they involve the "right" people (those most directly affected) in correct ways?
(d) *Accuracy:* Will the program evaluation yield valid and reliable results?

With all of these points in mind, let's consider the major components of evaluating a program's effects: (a) examine data to determine outcomes, (b) identify impacts and consider incidence, and (c) disseminate results.

Step 8: Examine outcome evaluation data to determine outcomes—process, analyze, and interpret data that are collected within an evaluation design to determine preventive effects of the program. *Assess changes in awareness, knowledge, attitudes, values, skills, behaviors, practices, and policies that are related to the problem statement, in preventive goals and objectives, and determine if any changes realized are sustainable over time.*

Outcome evaluation is concerned with identifying gains made by program participants and attempting to distinguish to what degree those gains (if any) were a consequence of program participation. Of typical import are assessments in the domains of knowledge, skills and behaviors, attitudes, and values.

Prevention programs need to be evaluated for numerous outcomes, including if new cases of problems diminished as a result of the prevention program.

Some of the many important summative evaluation questions include the following:

- Did the program reach its goals?
- Did participants realize gains in knowledge, skills and behaviors, values, and attitudes?

- Were deficits reduced?
- Was the environment improved?
- Were strengths and natural supports increased?
- Did the program make the difference it set out to make in participants?

In our overly simplified example, was school attendance increased by 10% after the program, with its four strategies, introduced? Were any other gains realized, such as improvements in the positive connection of students with the school?

To be able to demonstrate bottom-line effects, the prevention program needs to be set within the best research design possible for the circumstances. Community conditions often are not amenable to scientific research designs, of course. Still, program planners should aspire to use the classic research design of randomized experimental control with established measures whenever possible. Sometimes this is possible, often it is not for many reasons. But always start there, aim for it.

Examine research and evaluation designs of "model" programs that have been able to demonstrate evidence of success for ideas of how to begin producing the best possible design for your situation. Scale down to the next best design, then the next best, as conditions warrant. Qualitative designs emphasizing careful description will not be able to generalize beyond the local setting, but, depending on what is asked, these studies can reveal substantive information about how a particular program worked, how participants experienced the activities, and how they evolved. In fact, sometimes a qualitative design may best fit a particular situation. Combinations of quantitative and qualitative research designs can sometimes reflect the best of both worlds.

Sustainability of effects realized is an essential outcome matter. Demonstrated effectiveness is very important but it is not sufficient unless results are carried forward over time; that is, they are sustained. In this case, will improved attendance carry over in subsequent high school years? What plans have been made to extend effects, to enable participants to attain the necessary support and encouragement to maintain their gains? What changes have been made in the school environment to encourage and positively reinforce positive movement? Sometimes, as pointed out earlier, booster sessions can be helpful in prolonging learning and change. In terms of measurement, research designs can be established to include longer-term follow-up. And consideration needs to be given to creating programs and research designs that are longitudinal in scope, being able to endure over time.

Step 9: Identify impacts, incidence reduction. *Effects of outcomes: Assess larger changes in conditions, such as in health, social, political, economic, environmental, and civic domains, that are related to the problem statement, preventive goals and objectives, outcomes, and incidence reduction.*

Impact evaluation is a "big picture" endeavor. Essentially, as mentioned before, an impact is a fuller-scale outcome—in a sense, it is an effect of an outcome. If it could be shown that participants gained new skills in decision making as a result of program participation, how does that important skill affect their school attendance? How does improved decision making contribute to satisfaction with the school experience, with relationships with others, and over time with graduate rates? In a sense, outcomes are midstate end points, however confusing that may be to you. While important, realizing new relevant knowledge, more positive attitudes, values that are aligned with cooperation and diligence, and new skills in cooperative learning (all these are examples) do not mean that bottom-line prevention program goals will be met, such as improved attendance and incidence reduction of school failure. Nor do ostensibly positive changes in the school environment that may have been stimulated by the prevention program, such as a new mentoring program and additional school counselors and school nurses, necessarily translate into those same desired bottom-line goals.

So program impacts refer to deeper and broader changes being realized. For prevention programs, these often coalesce around incidence reduction, where new cases of a problem, disorder, or illness are stopped or reduced through intentional changes emerging in the competencies of people and through environmental adaptations and innovations.

Step 10: Disseminate results. *Communicate preventive results to pertinent audiences, both local and scientific (the latter, if warranted) in timely and usable ways and to allow for replication and adaptation by others.*

Dissemination of program processes and outcomes is a critically important issue deserving close consideration. Program personnel have an obligation to spread effective interventions. Related to transferability, above, dissemination is a step too few program personnel take. Once a program is finished and a report is filed, typical practice is that not much else may occur. This kind of "program abandonment" needs to change. Outcome evaluation should naturally include a dissemination phase, not just in funded projects but in all projects, where others can access program design, processes, outcomes, data, and recommendations. In this way, the storehouse of knowledge can be shared and expanded, leading to improved research and practice.

Dissemination connects directly with the scientific community. Effective and noneffective programs, as well, need to be published and presented in scientific outlets. The test might be if the science was done well. Statistically significant results are an important index of effectiveness. Yet, as pointed out earlier, clinical significance (or practical significance outside the clinical domain) also is important. We have much to learn from such projects.

Dissemination needs to be connected more closely with the practice community. Reliance on scientific publications and presentations will not reach most professional practitioners and hardly any other community workers. Efforts need to be conducted to disseminate, which often may mean to translate, program findings and procedures into local settings.

Replication, transferability, and usefulness are the next outcome issues. Indeed, if the program is deemed effective and sustainable and is disseminated, is it described in such a way as to be readily understood and applied?

Is the program described in enough detail that it could be implemented again (replicated) or be transferred for use in similar circumstances by others?

Imagine the program being parachuted down into another setting. What are the chances it could be implemented there? Would people there understand it? Is there enough information provided, so they could move ahead with adoption or, more likely, with adaptation? Program personnel need to describe their interventions and outcomes in sufficient detail so that others could readily understand and use them.

To conclude this chapter, let's review in a basic manner by attending to process and outcome and then looking back over your own personal prevention project you have been planning.

Learning Exercise 7: Defining Process and Outcome Evaluation

Process (or formative evaluation) and outcome (or summative evaluation) are both important in program evaluation.

- What is process evaluation? Provide a definition with two examples of *processes*.

  Definition: _____

  _____

  Example 1:_____

  Example 2: _____

- What is outcome evaluation? Give a definition with two examples of *outcomes*.

  Definition: _____

  _____

  Example 1:_____

  Example 2: _____

Take your own prevention topic. How would you incorporate attention to process and to outcome?

_____

_____

_____

> ## Learning Exercise 8: Examining Your Own Prevention Program
>
> Programs must be specifically planned with built-in procedures for monitoring and evaluating their success.
>
> Let's return to the prevention topic you have been working with as you've been moving through all these steps. Comment below on your ability to describe in concrete terms the *Problem–Objective–Strategies–Activities–Tasks–Timelines–Resources:*
>
>
> As you look at the relationship among all these linkages, jot notes to the following two questions:
>
> What could go wrong with my plan?
>
> What could I do to prevent those things from going wrong?

Summary

This final chapter is anchored by the role played by PD&E in *doing* prevention and in determining its value. A 10-step PD&E in Prevention plan is detailed, organized within the cyclical phases of planning, implementing, and effects.

Planning steps include the following: (1) lay groundwork for community, collaboration, and cultural relevance; (2) analyze local context and conduct professional literature review; (3) create problem statement; (4) develop preventive goals, objectives, strategies, and evaluation; and (5) obtain inputs and resources.

Implementation, including process evaluation steps, includes the following: (6) implement the program plan with participants through strategies, comprising sequenced and coordinated activities, tasks, responsibilities, resources, and timelines and (7) examine process evaluation and generate feedback.

The *Effects* phase, focused on evaluating outputs, includes the following: (8) examine output data to determine outcomes; (9) identify impacts and incidence reduction; and (10) disseminate results.

A lengthy example related to the problem of student absenteeism and attrition is provided to demonstrate how the 10-step plan can be applied.

Appendix A _____

The 10-Step PD&E in Prevention Model

A. **Plan the Program**

 1. Lay the groundwork for community, collaboration, and cultural relevance.

 2. Analyze local context and conduct professional literature review.

 3. Create problem statement.

 4. Develop preventive goals, objectives, strategies, and evaluations.

 5. Obtain inputs and resources.

B. **Implement, Including Process Evaluation**

 6. Implement program plan with participants through strategies comprising sequenced and coordinated activities, tasks, responsibilities, resources, and timelines.

 7. Examine process evaluation data to generate feedback.

C. **Effects: Evaluate Output**

 8. Examine outcome evaluation data to determine outcomes.

 9. Identify impacts, incidence reduction.

 10. Disseminate results.

Appendix B _____

Design the Prevention Program Implementation Plan

1. Determine problem

2. Set objectives

3. Choose among alternative strategies

4. Plan implementation

   Objectives

   Strategies

   Activities

   Tasks

   Responsibilities

   Resources

   Timelines

Appendix C _____

Design the Prevention Program Evaluation

Plan A. Process/Formative Evaluation

Key Processes

Community orientation

Cultural relevance/fit

Collaboration/partnerships

Fidelity

Evidence base

Key Evaluation Criteria

Context

Adequacy, appropriateness

Effectiveness, efficiency

Side effects, sustainability

Transferability, dissemination

Usefulness and general contribution

Plan B. Outcome/Summative Evaluation

Design process/formative evaluation

Design outcome/summative evaluation

Plan for sustainability

Plan for replication and transferability

Plan for dissemination and usefulness

Appendix D _____

Key Prevention Questions

Were new cases eliminated or diminished?

Were deficits reduced?

Was the environment improved?

Were strengths and natural supports increased?

References _____

Albee, G. (1982). Preventing psychopathology and promoting human potential. *American Psychologist, 37,* 1043–1050.

Albee, G. (1985). The argument for primary prevention. *Journal of Primary Prevention, 5,* 213–219.

Albee, G., & Gullotta, T. (Eds.). (1997). *Primary prevention works.* Thousand Oaks, CA: Sage.

Aldana, S., Merrill, R., Price, K., Hardy, A., & Hager, R. (2005). Financial impact of a comprehensive multisite workplace health promotion program. *Preventive Medicine, 40,* 131–137.

American Psychological Association. (2002). Guidelines on multicultural education, training, research, practice, and organization change for psychologists. *American Psychologist, 61,* 271–285. Retrieved from http://www.apa.org/pi/multicultural guidelines.pdf

American Psychological Association Presidential Task Force on Evidence-Based Practice. (2006). Evidence-based practice in psychology. *American Psychologist, 61,* 271–285.

Association for Specialists in Group Work. (1998). *Principles for diversity-competent group workers.* Retrieved from http://www.asgw.org/PDF/Principles_for_Diversity.pdf

Board of Regents. (2008). *Developing a logic model: Teaching and training guide. University of Wisconsin System.* Retrieved from http://www.uwex.edu/ces/pdande/evaluation/evallogicmodel.html

Bronfenbrenner, U. (1979). *The ecology of human development.* Cambridge, MA: Harvard University Press.

Center for the Study and Prevention of Violence. (2002–2004). *Blueprints for violence prevention.* Retrieved from http://www.colorado.edu/cspv/blueprints/

Centers for Disease Control and Prevention. (1999). Framework for program evaluation in public health. *Morbidity and Mortality Weekly Report, 48*(RR11), 1–40.

Centers for Disease Control and Prevention. (2005). *Child maltreatment prevention.* Retrieved from http://www.cdc.gov/ncipc/dvp/CMP/CMP-conque.htm

Chen, H.-T. (2005). *Practical program evaluation: Assessing and improving planning, implementation, and effectiveness.* Thousand Oaks, CA: Sage.

Cohen, L., Chavez, V., & Chehimi, S. (2010). *Prevention is primary: Strategies for community well-being.* San Francisco, CA: Jossey-Bass.

Coie, J., Watt, N., West, S., Hawkins, J., Asarnow, J., Markman, H., . . . Long, B. (1993). The science of prevention: A conceptual framework and some directions for a national research program. *American Psychologist, 48,* 1013–1022.

The Collaborative for Academic, Social, and Emotional Learning. (2003). *Safe and sound: An educational leader's guide to evidence-based social and emotional learning (SEL) programs.* Chicago, IL: Author.

The Collaborative for Academic, Social, and Emotional Learning. (2008). Retrieved from http://www.casel.org/

Conyne, R. (1989). *How personal growth and task groups work.* Newbury Park, CA: Sage.

Conyne, R. (2004). *Preventive counseling: Helping people to become empowered in systems and settings* (2nd ed.). New York, NY: Brunner-Routledge.

Conyne, R. (2010). *Prevention program development and evaluation: An incidence reduction, culturally relevant approach.* Thousand Oaks, CA: Sage.

Conyne, R., & Clack, R. J. (1981). *Environmental assessment and design: A new tool for the applied behavioral scientist.* New York, NY: Praeger.

Conyne, R., & Cook, E. (Eds.). (2004). *Ecological counseling: An innovative approach to conceptualizing person-environment interaction.* Alexandria, VA: American Counseling Association.

Conyne, R., Crowell, J., & Newmeyer, M. (2008). *Group techniques: How to use them more purposefully.* Upper Saddle River, NJ: Prentice Hall.

Conyne, R., Rapin, L., & Rand, J. (1997). A model for leading task groups. In H. Forester-Miller & J. Kottler (Eds.), *Issues and challenges for group practitioners* (pp. 117–132). Denver, CO: Love.

Craig, D. (1978). *HIP pocket guide to planning & evaluation.* Austin, TX: Learning Concepts.

Devaney, E., O'Brien, M., Resnik, H., Keister, S., & Weissberg, R. (2006). *Sustainable schoolwide social and emotional learning (SEL): Implementation guide and toolkit.* Chicago, IL: CASEL.

Elden, M., & Levin, M. (1991). Cogenerative learning: Bringing participation into action research. In W. F. Whyte (Ed.), *Participatory action research* (pp. 127–142). Newbury Park, CA: Sage.

Elias, M., O'Brien, M. U., & Weissberg, R. (2006). *Transformative leadership for social-emotional learning.* Retrieved from http://www.nasponline.org/resources/principals/Social%20Emotional%20Learning%20NASSP.pdf

Fujishin, R. (2001). *Creating effective groups: The art of small group communication.* San Francisco, CA: Acada Books.

Goldston, D., Molock, S. D., Whiteck, L., Murakami, J., Zayas, L., & Nagayama Hall, G. (2008). Cultural considerations in adolescent suicide prevention and psychosocial treatment. *American Psychologist, 63,* 14–31.

Green, L. (2007). *A resource for instructors, students, health practitioners, and researchers using the PRECEDE-PROCEED model for health program planning and evaluation.* Retrieved from http://www.lgreen.net/

Green, L., & Kreuter, M. (1999). *Health promotion planning: An educational and ecological approach* (3rd ed.). Mountain View, CA: Mayfield.

A group of brave otters vs. an alligator. (2011). Retrieved from http://www.pbs.org/wnet/nature/episodes/invasion-of-the-giant-pythons/video-alligator-vs-python/5541/

Gullotta, T., & Bloom, M. (Eds.). (2003). *Encyclopedia of primary prevention and health promotion.* New York, NY: Kluwer.

Hage, S., Romano, J., Conyne, R., Kenny, M., Matthews, C., Schwartz, J., & Waldo, M. (2007). Best practice guidelines on prevention practice, research, training, and social advocacy for psychologists. *The Counseling Psychologist, 35,* 493–566.

Holden, D., & Zimmerman, M. (Eds.). (2009). *A practical guide to program evaluation planning*. Thousand Oaks, CA: Sage.

Hulse-Killacky, D., Killacky, J., & Donigian, J. (2001). *Making task groups work in your world*. Upper Saddle River, NJ: Prentice Hall.

Institute of Medicine. (1994). *Reducing risks for mental disorder: Frontiers for preventive intervention research*. Washington, DC: National Academies Press.

Institute of Medicine. (2001). *Crossing the quality chasm: A new health system for the 21st century*. Washington, DC: National Academies Press.

Jacobson, M., & Rugeley, C. (2007). Community-based participatory research: Group work for social justice and community change. *Journal of Primary Prevention, 30*, 21–39.

Kazdin, A. (2008). Evidence-based treatment and practice: New opportunities to bridge clinical research and practice, enhance the knowledge base, and improve patient care. *American Psychologist, 63*, 146–159.

Kelly, J., & Hess, R. (Eds.). (1987). *The ecology of prevention: Illustrating mental health consultation*. New York, NY: Haworth.

Kenny, M., Horne, A., Orpinas, P., & Reese, L. (Eds.). *Realizing social justice: The challenge of preventive interventions*. Washington, DC: American Psychological Association.

Kessler, R., Heeringa, S., Lakoma, M. D., Petukhova, M., Rupp, A. E., Schoenbaum, M., . . . Zaslavsky, A. M. (2008). Individual and societal effects of mental disorders on earnings in the United States: Results from the national comorbidity survey replication. *American Journal of Psychiatry, 165*, 703–711.

Kettner, P., Moroney, R., & Martin, L. (2008). *Designing and managing programs: An effectiveness-based approach* (3rd ed.). Thousand Oaks, CA: Sage.

Keyes, C. (2002). The mental health continuum: From languishing to flourishing in life. *Journal of Health and Social Research, 43*, 207–222.

Lum, C. (2011, January 14). *ACA update: Student-to-counselor ratio remains high*. Retrieved from http://mail.google.com/mail/?hl=en&tab=wm#inbox/12d85143 d505fa07

Martin, J. (2011). *Schools watch court case on breast cancer bracelets*. Retrieved from http://www.usatoday.com/news/education/2011-01-12-bracelets12_ST_N.htm

Mertens, D. (2008). *Transformative research and evaluation*. New York, NY: Guilford Press.

Moore, M., & Delworth, U. (1976). *Training manual for student service program development*. Boulder, CO: WICHE.

Morrill, W., Oetting, E., & Hurst, J. (1974). Dimensions of counselor functioning. *Personnel and Guidance Journal, 52*, 354–359.

Norcross, J. (Ed.). (2002). *Psychotherapy relationships that work: Therapist contributions and responsiveness to patient needs*. New York, NY: Oxford University Press.

Office of Disease Prevention and Health Promotion. (2011). *Improve heart health*. Retrieved from http://mail.google.com/mail/#mbox/12e34551e7b0e748

Patton, M. Q. (1997). *Utilization-focused evaluation* (3rd ed.). Thousand Oaks, CA: Sage.

Paul, M. (2011). *Universities miss the chance to identify depressed students*. Retrieved from http://www.northwestern.edu/newscenter/stories/2011/01/depression-university-students.html

Perales, D. (2010). Primary prevention and evaluation. In L. Cohen, V. Chavez, & S. Chehimi (Eds.), *Prevention is primary: Strategies for community well-being* (2nd ed., pp. 205–229). San Francisco, CA: Jossey-Bass.

Reese, L., & Vera, E. (2007). Major contribution: Culturally-relevant prevention: The scientific and practical considerations of community-based programs. *The Counseling Psychologist, 35,* 763–778.

Riessman, F. (1965). The "helper" therapy principle. *Social Work, 10,* 27–32.

Rollnick, S., & Miller, W. R. (1995). What is motivational interviewing? *Behavioural and Cognitive Psychotherapy, 23,* 325–334.

Romano, J., & Hage, S. (2000). Major contribution: Prevention in counseling psychology. *The Counseling Psychologist, 28,* 733–763.

Sackett, D., Straus, S., Richardson, W., Rosenberg, W., & Haynes, R. (2000). Evidence-based medicine: What it is and what it isn't. *British Medical Journal, 31,* 71–72.

Savaya, R., & Waysman, M. (2005). The logic model: A tool for incorporating theory in development and evaluation of programs. *Administration in Social Work, 29,* 180–190.

Schwarz, R. (2002). *The skilled facilitator: A comprehensive resource for consultants, facilitators, manager, trainers, and coaches.* San Francisco, CA: Jossey-Bass.

Smith, E. (2006). Major contribution: The strength-based counseling model. *The Counseling Psychologist, 34,* 13–79.

Smith, L. (2005). Psychotherapy, classism, and the poor: Conspicuous by their absence. *American Psychologist, 60,* 687–696.

Smith, L. (2008). Positioning classism within counseling psychology's social justice agenda. *The Counseling Psychologist, 36,* 895–924.

Stufflebeam, D. (2003, October). *The CIPP model for evaluation.* Paper presented at the annual meeting of the Oregon Program Evaluators Network, Portland, Oregon. Retrieved from http://www.scribd.com/doc/58435354/The-Cipp-Model-for-Evaluation-by-Daniel-l-Stufflebeam

Sue, D. W., Arredondo, P., & McDavis, R. (1992). Multicultural counseling competencies and standards: A call to the profession. *Journal of Counseling & Development, 70,* 477–486.

Sue, S., Zane, N., & Young, K. (1994). Research on psychotherapy with culturally diverse populations. In A. Bergin & S. Garfield (Eds.), *Handbook of psychotherapy and behavior change* (4th ed., pp. 783–817). New York, NY: Wiley.

Tripodi, T., Fellin, P., & Epstein, I. (1978). *Differential social program evaluation.* Itasca, IL: Peacock.

U.S. Public Health Service. (2000). *Report of the Surgeon General's conference on children's mental health: A national action agenda.* Washington, DC: Department of Health and Human Services.

Vera, E. (2008, March). Commentary on the Choices program. In A. Horne (Chair), *Prevention practice: A workshop on prevention application programs that have demonstrated effectiveness.* Paper presented at the 2008 International Counseling Psychology Conference, Chicago, IL.

Vera, E., Caldwell, J., Clarke, M., Gonzales, R., Morgan, M., & West, M. (2007). The Choices program: Multisystemic interventions for enhancing the personal and academic effectiveness of urban adolescents of color. *The Counseling Psychologist, 35,* 779–796.

Wandersman, A., & Florin, P. (2003). Community interventions and effective prevention. *American Psychologist, 58,* 441–448.

Wang, P. S., Patrick, A., Avorn, J., Azocar, F., Ludman, E., McCulloch, J., . . . Kessler, R. (2006). The costs and benefits of enhanced depression care to employers. *Archives of General Psychiatry, 63,* 1345–1353.

Washington State Institute for Public Policy. (2004). *Benefits and costs of prevention and early intervention programs for youth*. Olympia: Washington State University.

Wells, A., Mance, G., Tirmazi, M. T., & Gone, J. (2010). Mental health in the realm of primary prevention. In L. Cohen, V. Chavez, & S. Chehimi (Eds.), *Prevention is primary: Strategies of community well-being* (pp. 370–405). San Francisco, CA: Jossey-Bass.

Wilson, M. (1950). *The music man*. New York, NY: Frank Music.

Wolfe, T. (1979). *The right stuff*. New York, NY: Farrar, Straus, & Giroux. Retrieved from www.aarpmagazine.org/lifestyle

Index _____

About the Author_____

Robert K. Conyne, PhD, Professor Emeritus from the University of Cincinnati, is a Licensed Psychologist, Clinical Counselor, and Fellow of the Association for Specialists in Group Work (ASGW) and the American Psychological Association. He compiled 36 years of professional experience as a University Professor and Department Head, counselor, administrator, consultant, and trainer. Dr. Conyne has received many awards, including Eminent Career Award from the ASGW; Lifetime Achievement Award in Prevention, Society of Counseling Psychology of the APA; Distinguished Alumni Award of Distinction from Purdue University, and a Soros International Scholar. He was President of the APA's Division of Group Psychology and Group Psychotherapy and also of the ACA's ASGW. With more than 200 scholarly publications and presentations including 12 books in his areas of expertise (group work, prevention, and ecological counseling), along with broad international consultation in these areas—most recently with U.S. military personnel, Dr. Conyne is recognized as an expert in working with people and systems. With colleague (and wife), Lynn S. Rapin, PhD, he also helps people plan and prepare psychologically for their upcoming retirement, using the holistic approach they developed, "Charting Your Personal Future." The edited *Oxford Handbook of Group Counseling* (2011) is his most recent offering, preceded by *Prevention Program Development and Evaluation* (Sage), and 12 other books. When not working, Dr. Conyne and his wife—as often as possible with their children Suzanne (married to Pete) and Zack—can be found traveling or enjoying life at their Northern Ontario cottage with their dog, Lucy.

ⓈSAGE research**methods**

The essential online tool for researchers from the world's leading methods publisher

Find exactly what you are looking for, from basic explanations to advanced discussion

More content and new features added this year!

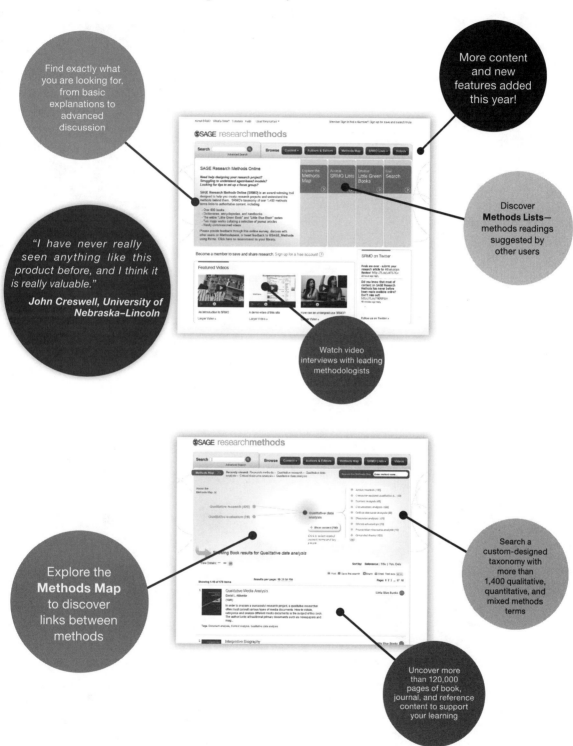

Discover **Methods Lists**— methods readings suggested by other users

"I have never really seen anything like this product before, and I think it is really valuable."

John Creswell, University of Nebraska–Lincoln

Watch video interviews with leading methodologists

Explore the **Methods Map** to discover links between methods

Search a custom-designed taxonomy with more than 1,400 qualitative, quantitative, and mixed methods terms

Uncover more than 120,000 pages of book, journal, and reference content to support your learning

Find out more at
www.sageresearchmethods.com